the end of imagination

The author's royalties have been assigned to
THE CAMPAIGN AGAINST NUCLEAR WEAPONS IN INDIA

the end of imagination

arundhati roy

D C BOOKS

DEECEE CONTEMPORARY SERIES

THE END OF IMAGINATION

ARUNDHATI ROY

Rights Reserved
First Published October 1998
Reprinted November 1998, September 1999

by

D C Books

Kottayam - 686 001, Kerala, India
Website : www.dcbooks.com
e-mail : dcbooksc@giasmd01.vsnl.net.in

ISBN 81 7130 867 8

PRINTED IN INDIA
at D C Offset Printers, Kottayam, Kerala, India - 686 001
186/99-00 3684 1946 2000 0999

Price Rs. 50.00

*For Marmots and Voles and everything else
on earth that is threatened and terrorised
by the human race*

Oh! for a life of the imagination

The proliferation of nuclear weapons threatens the very existence of mankind. In *The End of Imagination* Arundhati Roy's concern for humanity, threatened by self-brought calamity is expressed with great sincerity and depth of feeling. It is an inspired outburst against the sinister attempts at the dehumanization of man, the destruction of human civilisation and the self-aggrandisement of small-minded politicians. She forcefully condemns the perverse emphasis on national identity and national security by the leaders of a nation that has come nowhere near solving its problems of poverty and backwardness. Her unsentimental lament for the bleak future of humanity is heart-rending.

"My world has died. And I write to mourn its passing."

The author of the *The God of Small Things* once again writes about big things.

D C Books gratefully acknowledges the privilege of publishing the impassioned plea for peace in our time, in our world.

D C Kizhakemuri
Publisher

ACKNOWLEDGMENTS

N. Ram, Convenor, The Campaign Against Nuclear Weapons in India.
Photos
Pradeep Krishen
The Frontline
Gamma Presse Images, Vanves (Paris)
Hiroshima Nagasaki Publishing Committee
The Japan Council Against Atomic and Hydrogen Bombs, Edogawa Branch

"The desert shook," the Government of India informed us (its people).

"The whole mountain turned white," the Government of Pakistan replied.

By afternoon the wind had fallen silent over Pokhran. At 3.45 p.m., the timer detonated the three devices. Around 200 to 300 m deep in the earth, the heat generated was equivalent to a million degrees centigrade—as hot as temperatures on the sun. Instantly, rocks weighing around a thousand tons, a mini mountain underground, vapourised...shockwaves from the blast began to lift a mound of earth the size of a football field by several metres. One scientist on seeing it said, "I can now believe stories of Lord Krishna lifting a hill."

—India Today

May 1998. It'll go down in history books, provided, of course, we have history books to go down

9

in. Provided, of course, we have a future.

There's nothing new or original left to be said about nuclear weapons. There can be nothing more humiliating for a writer of fiction to have to do than restate a case that has, over the years, already been made by other people in other parts of the world, and made passionately, eloquently and knowledgeably.

I am prepared to grovel. To humiliate myself abjectly, because, in the circumstances, silence would be indefensible. So those of you who are willing: let's pick our parts, put on these discarded costumes and speak our second-hand lines in this

sad second-hand play. But let's not forget that the stakes we're playing for are huge. Our fatigue and our shame could mean the end of us. The end of our children and our children's children. Of everything we love. We have to reach within ourselves and find the strength to think. To fight.

Once again we are pitifully behind the times—not just scientifically and technologically (ignore the hollow claims), but more pertinently in our ability to grasp the true nature of nuclear weapons. Our Comprehension of the Horror Department is hopelessly obsolete. Here we are, all of us in India and in Pakistan, discussing the finer points of politics, and foreign policy, behaving for all the world as though our governments have just devised a newer, bigger bomb, a sort of immense hand grenade with which they will annihilate the enemy (each other) and protect us from all harm. How desperately we want to believe that. What wonderful, willing, well-behaved, gullible subjects we have turned out to be. The rest of humanity (Yes, yes, I know, I *know,* but let's ignore Them for the moment. They forfeited their votes a long time ago), the rest of the rest of humanity may not forgive us, but then the rest of the rest of humanity, depending on who fashions its views, may not know what a tired, dejected heart-broken people we are. Perhaps it doesn't realize how urgently we need a miracle. How deeply we yearn for magic.

If only, if *only,* nuclear war was just another kind of war. If only it was about the usual things—nations and territories, gods and histories. If only those of us who dread it are just worthless moral cowards who are not prepared to die in defence of our beliefs. If only nuclear war was the kind of war in which countries battle countries and men battle men. But it isn't. If there is a nuclear war,

our foes will not be China or America or even each other. Our foe will be the earth herself. The very elements—the sky, the air, the land, the wind and water—will all turn against us. Their wrath will be terrible.

Our cities and forests, our fields and villages will burn for days. Rivers will turn to poison. The air will become fire. The wind will spread the flames. When everything there is to burn has burned and the fires die, smoke will rise and shut out the sun. The earth will be enveloped in darkness. There will be no day. Only interminable night. Temperatures will drop to far below freezing and nuclear winter will set in. Water will turn into toxic ice. Radioactive fallout will seep through the earth and contaminate groundwater. Most living things, animal and vegetable, fish and fowl, will die. Only rats and cockroaches will breed and multiply and compete with foraging, relict humans for what little food there is.

What shall we do then, those of us who are still alive? Burned and blind and bald and ill, carrying the cancerous carcasses of our children in our arms, where shall we go? What shall we eat? What shall we drink? What shall we breathe?

The Head of the Health, Environment and Safety Group of the Bhabha Atomic Research Centre in Bombay has a plan. He declared in an interview (*The Pioneer*, April 24, 1998) that India could survive nuclear war. His advice is that if there is a nuclear war, we take the same safety measures as the ones that scientists have recommended in the event of accidents at nuclear plants.

Take iodine pills, he suggests. And other steps such as remaining indoors, consuming only stored water and food and avoiding milk. Infants should be given powdered milk. "People in the danger zone should immediately go to the ground floor and if possible to the basement."

What do you do with these levels of lunacy? What do you do if you're trapped in an asylum and the doctors are all dangerously deranged?

Ignore it, it's just a novelist's naivete, they'll

tell you, Doomsday Prophet hyperbole. It'll never come to that. There will *be* no war. Nuclear weapons are about peace, not war. 'Deterrence' is the buzz word of the people who like to think of themselves as hawks. (Nice birds, those. Cool. Stylish. Predatory. Pity there won't be many of them around after the war. Extinction is a word we must try and get used to.) Deterrence is an old thesis that has been resurrected and is being recycled with added local flavour. The Theory of Deterrence cornered the credit for having prevented the Cold War from turning into a Third World War. The only immutable fact about The Third World War is that if there's going to be one, it will be fought after the Second World War. In other words, there's no fixed schedule. In other words, we still have time. And perhaps the pun (The Third World War) is prescient. True, the Cold War is over, but let's not be hoodwinked by the ten-year lull in nuclear posturing. It was just a cruel joke. It was only in remission. It wasn't cured. It proves no theories. After all, what is ten years in the history of the world? Here it is again, the disease. More widespread and less amenable to any sort of treatment than ever. No, the Theory of Deterrence has some fundamental flaws.

Flaw Number One is that it presumes a complete, sophisticated understanding of the psychology of your enemy. It assumes that what deters you (the fear of annihilation) will deter them. What about those who are *not* deterred by that?

The suicide bomber psyche—the 'We'll take you with us' school—is that an outlandish thought? How did Rajiv Gandhi die?

In any case who's the 'you' and who's the 'enemy'? Both are only governments. Governments change. They wear masks within masks. They moult and re-invent themselves all the time. The one we have at the moment, for instance, does not even have enough seats to last a full term in office, but demands that we trust it to do pirouettes and party tricks with nuclear bombs even

as it scrabbles around for a foothold to maintain a simple majority in Parliament.

Flaw Number Two is that Deterrence is premised on fear. But fear is premised on knowledge. On an understanding of the true extent and scale of the devastation that nuclear war will wreak. It is not some inherent, mystical attribute of nuclear bombs that they automatically inspire thoughts of peace. On the contrary, it is the endless, tireless, confrontational work of people who have had the courage to openly denounce them, the marches, the demonstrations, the films, the outrage—*that* is what has averted, or perhaps only postponed, nuclear war. Deterrence will not and cannot work given the levels of ignorance and illiteracy that hang over our two countries like dense, impenetrable veils. (Witness the VHP wanting to distribute radioactive sand from the Pokhran desert as prasad all across India. A cancer yatra?) The Theory of Deterrence is nothing but a perilous joke in a world where iodine pills are prescribed as a prophylactic for nuclear irradiation.

India and Pakistan have nuclear bombs now and feel entirely justified in having them. Soon others will too. Israel, Iran, Iraq, Saudi Arabia, Norway, Nepal (I'm trying to be eclectic here), Denmark, Germany, Bhutan, Mexico, Lebanon, Sri Lanka, Burma, Bosnia, Singapore, North Korea, Sweden, South Korea, Vietnam, Cuba, Afghanistan, Uzbekistan...and why not? Every country in the world has a special case to make. Everybody has borders and beliefs. And when all our larders are bursting with shiny bombs and our bellies are empty (Deterrence is an exorbitant beast), we can trade bombs for food. And when nuclear technology goes on the market, when it gets truly competitive and prices fall, not just governments, but anybody who can afford it can have

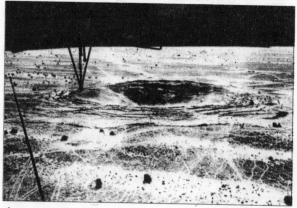

their own private arsenal—businessmen, terrorists, perhaps even the occasional rich writer (like myself). Our planet will bristle with beautiful missiles. There will be a new world order. The dictatorship of the pro-nuke elite. We can get our kicks by threatening each other. It'll be like bungee-jumping when you can't rely on the bungee cord, or playing Russian roulette all day long. An additional perk will be the thrill of Not Knowing What To Believe. We can be victims of the predatory imagination of every green card seeking charlatan who surfaces in the West with concocted stories of imminent missile attacks. We can delight at the prospect of being held to ransom by every petty trouble-maker and rumour-monger, the more the merrier if truth be told, anything for an excuse to make more bombs. So you see, even without a war, we have a lot to look forward to.

But let us pause to give credit where it's due. Whom must we thank for all this?

The Men who made it happen. The Masters of the Universe. Ladies and gentlemen, The United States of America! Come on up here folks, stand up and take a bow. Thankyou for doing this to the world. Thankyou for making a difference. Thankyou for showing us the way. Thankyou for altering the very meaning of life.

From now on it is not dying we must fear, but living.

It is such supreme folly to believe that nuclear weapons are deadly only if they're used. The fact that they exist at all, their very presence in our lives, will wreak more havoc than we can begin to fathom. Nuclear weapons pervade our thinking. Control our behaviour. Administer our societies. Inform our dreams. They bury themselves like meat hooks deep in the base of our brains. They are purveyors of madness. They are the ultimate coloniser. Whiter than any white man that ever lived. The very heart of whiteness.

All I can say to every man, woman and sentient child here in India, and over there, just a little way away in Pakistan, is: Take it personally. Whoever you are—Hindu, Muslim, urban, agrarian—it doesn't matter. The only good thing about nuclear war is that it is the single most egalitarian idea that man has ever had. On the day of reckoning, you will not be asked to present your credentials. The devastation will be indiscrimi-

nate. The bomb isn't in your backyard. It's in your body. And mine. *Nobody*, no nation, no government, no man, no god, has the right to put it there. We're radioactive already, and the war hasn't even begun. So stand up and say something. Never mind if it's been said before. Speak up on your own behalf. Take it very personally.

THE BOMB AND I

In early May (before the bomb), I left home for three weeks. I thought I would return. I had every intention of returning. Of course, things haven't worked out quite the way I had planned.

While I was away, I met a friend of mine whom I have always loved for, among other things, her ability to combine deep affection with a frankness that borders on savagery.

"I've been thinking about you," she said, "about *The God of Small Things*—what's in it, what's over it, under it, around it, above it..."

She fell silent for a while. I was uneasy and not at all sure that I wanted to hear the rest of what she had to say. She, however, was sure that she was going to say it. "In this last year—less than a year actually—you've had too much of everything—fame, money, prizes, adulation, criticism, condemnation, ridicule, love, hate, anger, envy, generosity—everything. In some ways it's a perfect story. Perfectly baroque in its excess. The trouble is that it has or can have, only one perfect ending." Her eyes were on me, bright with a slanting, probing brilliance. She knew that I knew what she was going to say. She was insane.

She was going to say that nothing that happened to me in the future could ever match the buzz of this. That the whole of the rest of my life was going to be vaguely unsatisfying. And, therefore, the only perfect ending to the story would be death. My death.

The thought had occurred to me too. Of course it had. The fact that all this, this global dazzle—these lights in my eyes, the applause, the flowers, the photographers, the journalists feigning a deep interest in my life (yet struggling to get a single fact straight), the men in suits fawning over me, the shiny hotel bathrooms with endless towels—none of it was likely to happen again. Would I miss it? Had I grown to need it? Was I a fame-junkie? Would I have withdrawal symptoms?

The more I thought about it, the clearer it became to me that if fame was going to be my permanent condition it would kill me. Club me to death with its good manners and hygiene. I'll admit that I've enjoyed my own five minutes of it immensely, but primarily *because* it was just five minutes. Because I knew (or thought I knew) that I could go home when I was bored and giggle about it. Grow old and irresponsible. Eat mangoes in the moonlight. Maybe write a couple of failed books—worstsellers—to see what it felt like. For a whole year I've cartwheeled across the world, anchored always to thoughts of home and the life I would go back to. Contrary to all the enquiries and predictions about my impending emigration, that was the well I dipped into. That was my sustenance. My strength.

I told my friend there was no such thing as a perfect story. I said in any case hers was an external view of things, this assumption that the trajectory of a person's happiness, or let's say fulfilment, had peaked (and now must trough) because she had accidentally stumbled upon 'success'. It was premised on the unimaginative belief that wealth and fame were the mandatory stuff of everybody's dreams.

You've lived too long in New York, I told her. There are other worlds. Other kinds of dreams. Dreams in which failure is feasible. Honourable. Sometimes even worth striving for. Worlds in which recognition is not the only barometer of brilliance or human worth. There are plenty of warriors that I know and love, people far more valuable than myself, who go to war each day, knowing in advance that they will fail. True, they are less 'successful' in the most vulgar sense of the word, but by no means less fulfilled.

23

The only dream worth having, I told her, is to dream that you will live while you're alive and die only when you're dead. (Prescience? Perhaps.)

"Which means exactly what?" (Arched eyebrows, a little annoyed.)

I tried to explain, but didn't do a very good job of it. Sometimes I need to write to think. So I wrote it down for her on a paper napkin. This is what I wrote: *To love. To be loved. To never forget your own insignificance. To never get used to the unspeakable violence and the vulgar disparity of life around you. To seek joy in the saddest places. To pursue beauty to its lair. To never simplify what is complicated or complicate what is simple. To respect strength, never power. Above all, to watch. To try and understand. To never look away. And never, never to forget.*

I've known her for many years, this friend of mine. She's an architect too.

She looked dubious, somewhat unconvinced by my paper napkin speech. I could tell that structurally, just in terms of the sleek, narrative symmetry of things, and because she loves me, her thrill at my 'success' was so keen, so generous, that it weighed in evenly with her (anticipated) horror at the idea of my death. I understood that

24

it was nothing personal. Just a design thing.

Anyhow, two weeks after that conversation, I returned to India. To what I think/thought of as home. Something had died but it wasn't me. It was infinitely more precious. It was a world that has been ailing for a while, and has finally breathed its last. It's been cremated now. The air is thick with ugliness and there's the unmistakable stench of fascism on the breeze.

Day after day, in newspaper editorials, on the radio, on TV chat shows, on MTV for heaven's sake, people whose instincts one thought one

could trust—writers, painters, journalists—make the crossing. The chill seeps into my bones as it becomes painfully apparent from the lessons of everyday life that what you read in history books is true. That fascism is indeed as much about people as about governments. That it begins at home. In drawing rooms. In bedrooms. In beds. "Explosion of self-esteem", "Road to Resurgence", "A Moment of Pride", these were headlines in the papers in the days following the nuclear tests. "We have proved that we are not eunuchs any more," said Mr Thackeray of the Shiv Sena. (Whoever said we were? True, a good number of us are women, but that, as far as I know, isn't the same thing.) Reading the papers, it was often hard to tell when people were referring to Viagra (which was competing for second place on the front pages) and when they were talking about the bomb— "We have superior strength and potency." (This was our Minister for Defence after Pakistan completed its tests.)

"These are not just nuclear tests, they are nationalism tests," we were repeatedly told.

This has been hammered home, over and over again. The bomb is India. India is the bomb. Not just India, Hindu India. Therefore, be warned, any criticism of it is not just anti-national, but anti-Hindu. (Of course, in Pakistan the bomb is Islamic. Other than that, politically, the same physics applies.) This is one of the unexpected perks of having a nuclear bomb. Not only can the Government use it to threaten the Enemy, they can use it to declare war on their own people. Us.

26

In 1975, one year after India first dipped her toe into the nuclear sea, Mrs Gandhi declared the Emergency. What will 1999 bring? There's talk of cells being set up to monitor anti-national activity. Talk of amending cable laws to ban net-

works 'harming national culture' (*The Indian Express*, July 3). Of churches being struck off the list of religious places because 'wine is served' (announced and retracted, *The Indian Express*, July 3, *The Times of India*, July 4). Artists, writers, actors, and singers are being harassed, threatened (and succumbing to the threats). Not just by goon squads, but by instruments of the government. And in courts of law. There are letters and articles circulating on the Net—creative interpretations of Nostradamus' predictions claiming that a mighty, all-conquering Hindu nation is about to emerge—a resurgent India that will "burst forth upon its former oppressors and destroy them completely." That "the beginning of the terrible revenge (that will wipe out all Moslems) will be in the seventh month of 1999." This may well be the work of some lone nut, or a bunch of arcane god-squadders. The trouble is that having a nuclear bomb makes thoughts like these seem feasible. It creates thoughts like these. It bestows on people these utterly misplaced, utterly deadly notions of their own power. It's happening. It's all happening. I wish I could say 'slowly but surely'—but I can't. Things are moving at a pretty fair clip.

Why does it all seem so familiar? Is it because, even as you watch, reality dissolves and seamlessly rushes forward into the silent, black and white images from old films—scenes of people being hounded out of their lives, rounded up and

28

herded into camps. Of massacre, of mayhem, of endless columns of broken people making their way to nowhere? Why is there no sound-track? Why is the hall so quiet? Have I been seeing too many films? Am I mad? Or am I right? Could those images be the inevitable culmination of what we have set into motion? Could our future be rushing forward into our past? I think so. Unless, of course, nuclear war settles it once and for all.

When I told my friends that I was writing this piece, they cautioned me. "Go ahead," they said, "but first make sure you're not vulnerable. Make sure your papers are in order. Make sure your taxes are paid."

My papers are in order. My taxes are paid. But how can one not be vulnerable in a climate like this? Everyone is vulnerable. Accidents happen. There's safety only in acquiescence. As I write, I am filled with foreboding. In this country, I have truly known what it means for a writer to feel loved (and, to some degree, hated too). Last year I was one of the items being paraded in the media's end-of-the-year National Pride Parade. Among the others, much to my mortification, were a bomb-maker and an international beauty queen. Each time a beaming person stopped me on the street and said 'You have made India proud' (referring to the prize I won, not the book I wrote), I felt a little uneasy. It frightened me then and it terrifies me now, because I know how easily that swell, that tide of emotion, can turn against me. Perhaps the time for that has come. I'm going to step out from under the fairy lights and say what's on my mind.

It's this:

If protesting against having a nuclear bomb implanted in my brain is anti-Hindu and anti-national, then I secede. I hereby declare myself an independent, mobile republic. I am a citizen of the earth. I own no territory. I have no flag. I'm female, but have nothing against eunuchs. My policies are simple. I'm willing to sign any nuclear non-proliferation treaty or nuclear test ban treaty that's going. Immigrants are welcome. You can help me design our flag.

My world has died. And I write to mourn its passing.

Admittedly it was a flawed world. An unviable world. A scarred and wounded world. It was a world that I myself have criticised unsparingly, but only because I loved it. It didn't deserve to die. It didn't deserve to be dismembered. Forgive

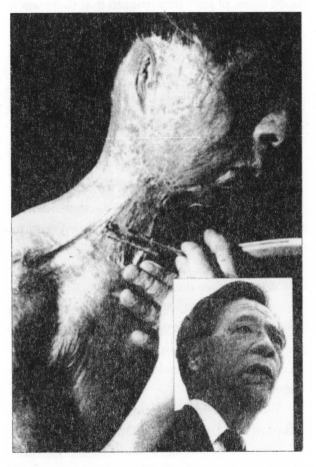

me, I realise that sentimentality is uncool--but what shall I do with my desolation?

I loved it simply because it offered humanity a choice. It was a rock out at sea. It was a stubborn chink of light that insisted that there was a different way of living. It was a functioning possibility. A real option. All that's gone now. India's nuclear tests, the manner in which they were conducted, the euphoria with which they have been greeted (by us) is indefensible. To me, it signifies dreadful things. The end of imagination. The end of freedom actually, because, after all, that's what freedom is. Choice.

On the 15th of August last year we celebrated the fiftieth anniversary of India's independence. Next May we can mark our first anniversary in nuclear bondage.

Why did they do it?

Political expediency is the obvious, cynical answer, except that it only raises another, more basic question: Why should it have been politically expedient?

The three Official Reasons given are: China, Pakistan and Exposing Western Hypocrisy.

Taken at face value, and examined individually, they're somewhat baffling. I'm not for a moment suggesting that these are not real issues. Merely that they aren't new. The only new thing on the old horizon is the Indian Government. In his appallingly cavalier letter to the US President (why bother to write at all if you're going to write like this?) our Prime Minister says India's decision to go ahead with the nuclear tests was due to a "deteriorating security environment". He goes on to mention the war with China in 1962 and the "three aggressions we have suffered in the last fifty years (from Pakistan). And for the last ten years we have been the victim of unremitting terrorism and militancy sponsored by it...especially in Jammu and Kashmir."

The war with China is thirty-five years old. Unless there's some vital state secret that we don't know about, it certainly seemed as though matters had improved slightly between us. Just a few days before the nuclear tests General Fu Quanyou, Chief of General Staff of the Chinese People's Liberation Army, was the guest of our Chief of Army Staff. We heard no words of war.

The most recent war with Pakistan was fought twenty-seven years ago. Admittedly Kashmir continues to be a deeply troubled region and no doubt Pakistan is gleefully fanning the flames. But surely there must be flames to fan in the first place? Surely the kindling is crackling and ready to burn? Can the Indian State with even a modicum of honesty absolve itself completely of having a hand in Kashmir's troubles? Kashmir, and for that matter, Assam, Tripura, Nagaland—virtually the whole of the Northeast—Jharkhand, Uttarakhand and all the trouble that's still to come—these are symptoms of a deeper malaise. It cannot and will not be solved by pointing nuclear missiles at Pakistan.

Even Pakistan can't be solved by pointing nuclear missiles at Pakistan. Though we are separate countries, we share skies, we share winds, we share water. Where radioactive fallout will land on any given day depends on the direction of the wind and rain. Lahore and Amritsar are thirty miles apart. If we bomb Lahore, Punjab will burn. If we bomb Karachi—then Gujarat and Rajasthan, perhaps even Bombay, will burn. Any nuclear war with Pakistan will be a war against ourselves.

As for the third Official Reason: Exposing Western Hypocrisy—how much more exposed can they be? Which decent human being on earth harbours any illusions about it? These are people whose histories are spongy with the blood of others. Colonialism, apartheid, slavery, ethnic cleansing, germ warfare, chemical weapons—they virtually invented it all. They have plundered nations, snuffed out civilisations, exterminated entire populations. They stand on the world's stage stark naked but entirely unembarrassed, because they know that they have more money, more food and bigger bombs than anybody else. They know they can wipe us out in the course of an ordinary working day. Personally, I'd say it is more arrogance than hypocrisy.

We have less money, less food and smaller bombs. However, we have, or had, all kinds of other wealth. Delightful, unquantifiable. What we've done with it is the opposite of what we think we've done. We've pawned it all. We've traded it in. For what? In order to enter into a contract with the very people we claim to despise. In the larger scheme of things, we've agreed to play their game and play it their way. We've accepted their terms and conditions unquestioningly. The CTBT ain't nothin' compared to this.

All in all, I think it is fair to say that *we're* the hypocrites. We're the ones who've abandoned what was arguably a moral position, i.e.: *We have the technology, we can make bombs if we want to, but we won't. We don't believe in them.*

We're the ones who have now set up this craven clamouring to be admitted into the club of Superpowers. (If we are, we will no doubt gladly slam the door after us, and say to hell with principles about fighting Discriminatory World Orders.) For India to demand the status of a Superpower is as ridiculous as demanding to play in the World Cup finals simply because we have a ball. Never mind that we haven't qualified, or that we don't play much soccer and haven't got a team.

Since we've chosen to enter the arena, it might be an idea to begin by learning the rules of the game. Rule number one is Acknowledge the Masters. Who are the best players? The ones with more money, more food, more bombs.

Rule number two is Locate Yourself in Relation to Them, i.e.: Make an honest assessment of your position and abilities. The honest assessment of ourselves (in quantifiable terms) reads as follows:

We are a nation of nearly a billion people. In development terms we rank No. 138 out of the 175 countries listed in the UNDP's Human Development Index. More than 400 million of our people are illiterate and live in absolute poverty, over 600 million lack even basic sanitation and over 200 million have no safe drinking water.

So the three Official Reasons, taken individually, don't hold much water. However, if you link them, a kind of twisted logic reveals itself. It has more to do with us than them.

The key words in our Prime Minister's letter

to the US President were 'suffered' and 'victim'. That's the substance of it. That's our meat and drink. We *need* to feel like victims. We need to feel beleaguered. We need enemies. We have so little sense of ourselves as a nation and therefore constantly cast about for targets to define ourselves against. Prevalent political wisdom suggests that to prevent the State from crumbling, we need a national cause, and other than our currency (and, of course, poverty, illiteracy and elections), we have none. This is the heart of the matter. This is the road that has led us to the bomb. This search for selfhood. If we are looking for a way out, we need some honest answers to some uncomfortable questions. Once again, it isn't as though these questions haven't been asked before. It's just that we prefer to mumble the answers and hope that no one's heard.

Is there such a thing as an Indian identity?
Do we really need one?
Who is an authentic Indian and who isn't?
Is India Indian?
Does it matter?

Whether or not there has ever been a single civilisation that could call itself 'Indian Civilisation', whether or not India was, is, or ever will become a cohesive cultural entity, depends on whether you dwell on the differences or the similarities in the cultures of the people who have inhabited the subcontinent for centuries. India, as a modern nation state, was marked out with precise geographical boundaries, in their precise geographical way, by a British Act of Parliament in 1899. Our country, as we know it, was forged on the anvil of the British Empire for the entirely unsentimental reasons of commerce and administration. But even as she was born, she began her struggle against her creators. So is India Indian? It's a tough question. Let's just say that we're an ancient people learning to live in a recent nation.

What is true is that India is an artificial State— a State that was created by a government, not a people. A State created from the top down, not the bottom up. The majority of India's citizens will not (to this day) be able to identify her boundaries on a map, or say which language is spoken where or which god is worshipped in what region. Most are too poor and too uneducated to have even an elementary idea of the extent and complexity of their own country. The impoverished, illiterate agrarian majority have no stake in the State. And indeed, why should they, how can they, when they don't even know what the

State is? To them, India is, at best, a noisy slogan that comes around during the elections. Or a montage of people on Government TV programmes wearing regional costumes and saying *Mera Bharat Mahan*.

The people who have a vital stake (or, more to the point, a business interest) in India having a single, lucid, cohesive national identity are the politicians who constitute our national political parties. The reason isn't far to seek, it's simply because their struggle, their career goal, is—and must necessarily be—to *become* that identity. To be identified with that identity. If there isn't one, they have to manufacture one and persuade people to vote for it. It isn't their fault. It comes with the territory. It is inherent in the nature of our system of centralised government. A congenital defect in our particular brand of democracy. The greater the numbers of illiterate people, the poorer the country and the more morally bankrupt the politicians, the cruder the ideas of what that identity should be. In a situation like this, illiteracy is not just sad, it's downright dangerous. However, to be fair, cobbling together a viable pre-digested 'National Identity' for India would be a formidable challenge even for the wise and the visionary. Every single Indian citizen could, if he or she wants to, claim to belong to some minority or the other. The fissures, if you look for them, run vertically, horizontally, layered, whorled, circular, spiral, inside out and outside in. Fires when they're lit race along any one of these schisms, and in the process, release tremendous bursts of political energy. Not unlike what happens when you split an atom.

It is this energy that Gandhi sought to harness when he rubbed the magic lamp and invited

Ram and Rahim to partake of human politics and India's war of independence against the British. It was a sophisticated, magnificent, imaginative struggle, but its objective was simple and lucid, the target highly visible, easy to identify and succulent with political sin. In the circumstances, the energy found an easy focus. The trouble is that the circumstances are entirely changed now, but the genie is out of its lamp, and won't go back in. (It could be sent back, but nobody wants it to go, it's proved itself too useful.) Yes, it won us freedom. But it also won us the carnage of Partition. And now, in the hands of lesser statesmen, it has won us the Hindu Nuclear Bomb.

To be fair to Gandhi and to other leaders of the National Movement, they did not have the benefit of hindsight, and could not possibly have known what the eventual, long-term consequences of their strategy would be. They could not have predicted how quickly the situation would career out of control. They could not have foreseen what would happen when they passed their flaming torches into the hands of their successors, or how venal those hands could be.

It was Indira Gandhi who started the real slide. It is she who made the genie a permanent State Guest. She injected the venom into our political veins. She invented our particularly vile local brand of political expediency. She showed us how to conjure enemies out of thin air, to fire at phantoms that she had carefully fashioned for that very purpose. It was she who discovered the benefits of never burying the dead, but preserving their putrid carcasses and trundling them out to worry old wounds when it suited her. Between herself and her sons she managed to bring the

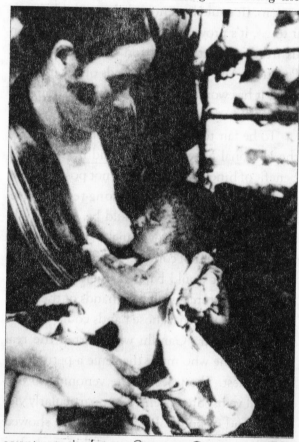

country to its knees. Our new Government has just kicked us over and arranged our heads on the chopping block.

The BJP is, in some senses, a spectre that

Indira Gandhi and the Congress created. Or, if you want to be less harsh, a spectre that fed and reared itself in the political spaces and communal suspicion that the Congress nourished and cultivated. It has put a new complexion on the politics of governance. While Mrs Gandhi played hidden games with politicians and their parties, she reserved a shrill convent school rhetoric, replete with tired platitudes, to address the general public. The BJP, on the other hand, has chosen to light its fires directly on the streets and in the homes and hearts of people. It is prepared to do by day what the Congress would do only by night. To legitimise what was previously considered unacceptable (but done anyway). There is perhaps a fragile case to be made here in favour of hypocrisy. Could the hypocrisy of the Congress Party, the fact that they conduct their wretched affairs surreptitiously instead of openly, could that possibly mean there is a tiny glimmer of guilt somewhere? Some small fragment of remembered decency?

Actually, no.

No.

What am I doing? Why am I foraging for scraps of hope?

The way it has worked—in the case of the

demolition of the Babri Masjid as well as in the making of the nuclear bomb—is that the Congress sowed the seeds, tended the crop, then the BJP stepped in and reaped the hideous harvest. They waltz together, locked in each others' arms. They're inseparable, despite their professed differences. Between them they have brought us here, to this dreadful, dreadful place.

The jeering, hooting young men who battered down the Babri Masjid are the same ones whose pictures appeared in the papers in the days that followed the nuclear tests. They were on the streets, celebrating India's nuclear bomb and simultaneously 'condemning Western Culture' by emptying crates of Coke and Pepsi into public drains. I'm a little baffled by their logic: Coke is

Western Culture, but the nuclear bomb is an old Indian tradition?

Yes, I've heard—the bomb is in the Vedas. It might be, but if you look hard enough, you'll find Coke in the Vedas too. That's the great thing about all religious texts. You can find anything you want in them—as long as you know what you're looking for.

But returning to the subject of the non-vedic nineteen nineties: We storm the heart of whiteness, we embrace the most diabolical creation of western science and call it our own. But we protest against their music, their food, their clothes, their cinema and their literature. That's not hypocrisy. That's humour.

It's funny enough to make a skull smile.

We're back on the old ship. The S.S. Authenticity & Indianness.

If there is going to be a pro-authenticity/anti-national drive, perhaps the government ought to get its history straight and its facts right. If they're going to do it, they may as well do it properly.

First of all, the original inhabitants of this land were not Hindu. Ancient though it is, there were human beings on earth before there was Hinduism. India's tribal people have a greater claim to being indigenous to this land than anybody else, and how are they treated by the State and its minions? Oppressed, cheated, robbed of their lands, shunted around like surplus goods. Perhaps a good place to start would be to restore to them the dignity that was once theirs. Perhaps the Government could make a public undertaking that more dams like the Sardar Sarovar on the Narmada will not be built, that more people will not be displaced.

But, of course, that would be inconceivable, wouldn't it? Why? Because it's impractical. Because tribal people don't really matter. Their histories, their customs, their deities are dispensable. They must learn to sacrifice these things for the greater good of the Nation (that has snatched from them everything they ever had).

Okay, so that's out.

For the rest, I could compile a practical list of things to ban and buildings to break. It'll need some research, but off the top of my head, here are a few suggestions.

They could begin by banning a number of ingredients from our cuisine: chillies (Mexico), tomatoes (Peru), potatoes (Bolivia), coffee (Morocco), tea, white sugar, cinnamon (China)...they could then move into recipes. Tea with milk and sugar, for instance (Britain).

Smoking will be out of the question. Tobacco came from North America.

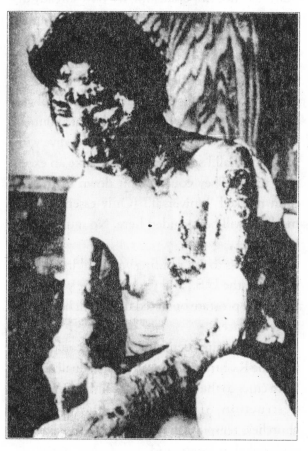

Cricket, English and Democracy should be forbidden. Either kabaddi or kho-kho could replace cricket. I don't want to start a riot, so I hesitate to suggest a replacement for English (Italian...? It has found its way to us via a kinder route: Marriage, not Imperialism). We have already discussed (earlier in this essay) the emerging, apparently acceptable alternative to democracy.

All hospitals in which western medicine is practised or prescribed should be shut down. All national newspapers discontinued. The railways dismantled. Airports closed. And what about our newest toy—the mobile phone? Can we live without it, or shall I suggest that they make an exception there? They could put it down in the column marked 'Universal'? (Only essential commodities will be included here. No music, art or literature.)

Needless to say, sending your children to university in the U.S., and rushing there yourself to have your prostate operated upon will be a cognizable offence.

The building demolition drive could begin with the Rashtrapati Bhavan and gradually spread from cities to the countryside, culminating in the destruction of all monuments (mosques, churches, temples) that were built on what was once tribal or forest land.

It will be a long, long list. It would take years of work. I couldn't use a computer because that wouldn't be very authentic of me, would it?

I don't mean to be facetious, merely to point out that this is surely the shortcut to hell. There's no such thing as an Authentic India or a Real Indian. There is no Divine Committee that has the right to sanction one single, authorised version of what India is or should be. There is no one religion or language or caste or region or person or story or book that can claim to be its sole representative. There are, and can only be, visions of India, various ways of seeing it—honest, dishonest, wonderful, absurd, modern, traditional, male, female. They can be argued over, criticised, praised, scorned, but not banned or broken. Not hunted down.

Railing against the past will not heal us. History has *happened*. It's over and done with. All we can do is to change its course by encouraging what we love instead of destroying what we don't. There is beauty yet in this brutal, damaged world of ours. Hidden, fierce, immense. Beauty that is uniquely ours and beauty that we have received with grace from others, enhanced, re-invented and made our own. We have to seek it out, nurture it, love it. Making bombs will only destroy us. It doesn't *matter* whether we use them or not. They will destroy us either way.

India's nuclear bomb is the final act of betrayal by a ruling class that has failed its people.

However many garlands we heap on our scientists, however many medals we pin to their chests, the truth is that it's far easier to make a bomb than to educate four hundred million people.

According to opinion polls, we're expected to believe that there's a national consensus on the issue. It's official now. Everybody loves the bomb. (Therefore the bomb is good.)

Is it possible for a man who cannot write his own name to understand even the basic, elementary facts about the nature of nuclear weapons? Has anybody told him that nuclear war has nothing at all to do with his received notions of war? Nothing to do with honour, nothing to do with pride. Has anybody bothered to explain to him about thermal blasts, radioactive fallout and the nuclear winter? Are there even words in his language to describe the concepts of enriched uranium, fissile material and critical mass? Or has his language itself become obsolete? Is he trapped in a time capsule, watching the world pass him by, unable to understand or communicate with it because his language never took into account the horrors that the human race would dream up? Does he not matter at all, this man? Shall we just treat him like some kind of a cretin? If he asks any questions, ply him with iodine pills and parables about how Lord Krishna lifted a hill or how the destruction of Lanka by Hanuman was

unavoidable in order to preserve Sita's virtue and Ram's reputation? Use his own beautiful stories as weapons against him? Shall we release him from his capsule only during elections, and once he's voted, shake him by the hand, flatter him with some bullshit about the Wisdom of the Common Man, and send him right back in?

I'm not talking about one man, of course, I'm talking about millions and millions of people who live in this country. This is their land too, you know. They have the right to make an informed decision about its fate and, as far as I can tell, nobody has informed them about anything. The tragedy is that nobody could, even if they wanted to. Truly, literally, there's no language to do it in. This is the real horror of India. The orbits of the powerful and the powerless spinning further and further apart from each other, never intersecting, sharing nothing. Not a language. Not even a country.

Who the hell conducted those opinion polls? Who the hell is the Prime Minister to decide whose finger will be on the nuclear button that could turn everything we love—our earth, our skies, our mountains, our plains, our rivers, our cities and villages —to ash in an instant? Who the hell is he to reassure us that there will be no accidents? How does he know? Why should we trust him? What has he ever done to make us trust him? What have any of them ever done to make us trust them?

The nuclear bomb is the most anti-democratic, anti-national, anti-human, outright evil thing that man has ever made.

If you are religious, then remember that this bomb is Man's challenge to God.

It's worded quite simply: *We have the power to destroy everything that You have created.*

If you're not (religious), then look at it this way. This world of ours is four thousand, six hundred million years old.

It could end in an afternoon.

oo

Index

'A Moment of Pride' 26
Acknowledge the Masters 36
Afghanistan 17
amending cable laws 27
Amritsar 34
anti-Hindu 26-30
apartheid 34
Assam 34
Authentic India 49
authentic Indian 37
Babri Masjid 44
Bhabha Atomic Research
    Centre 13
Bhutan 17
B J P 42, 43, 44
Bolivia 46
bomb-maker 29
Bosnia 17
British Act of
    Parliament (1899) 38
building demolition drive 48
bungee - jumping 18
Burma 17
cancer yatra 17
cancerous carcasses of children 13
chemical weapons 34
Chief of Army Staff 33
chillies 46
China 12,32
Chinese People's
    Liberation Army 33
churches 48
cinnamon 46
citizen of the earth 30
cockroaches 13
coffee 46
Cold war 15
colonialism 34
'condemning Western Culture' 44
Congress 43,44
Coke 44,45

countries battle countries 12
critical mass 50
CTBT 35
Cuba 17
Denmark 17
destruction of monuments 48
'deteriorating security
    environment' 33
Deterrence 15,16,18
devastation 20
Discriminatory World Orders 35
Divine Committee 49
Emergency 27
enriched uranium 50
Environment and Safety Group 13
ethnic cleansing 34
'Explosion of self-esteem' 26
Extinction 15
fame junkie 22
fascism 25
fiftieth anniversary of
    India's independence 32
fissile material 50
fundamental flaws 15,16-17
Fu Quanyou, General 33
Gandhi, Indira 27,41,42,43
Gandhi, Mahatma 40,41
Gandhi, Rajiv 16
germ warfare 34
Germany 17
global dazzle 22
god-squdders 28
goon squads 28
Gujarat 34
hand grenade 11
Hindu India 26
Hindu Nuclear Bomb 41
Hinduism 45
Horror Department 11
Human Development Index 36
Imperialism 48
Immigrants 30

India 9,11,13,17, 20,25,26 ,
27,30,36,37,38,39,52
India Today 9
India's war of independence 40
'Indian Civilisation' 37
Indian identity 37
infants 13
interminable night 12
international beauty queen 29
iodine pills 13,25,51
Iran 17
Iraq 17
Islamic Bomb 26
Israel 17
Jammu 33
Jharkhand 34
kabaddi 47
Karachi 44
Kashmir 33,44
kho-kho 47
Lahore 34
Lebanon 17
Locate Yours in relation
to Them 36
Lord Krishna 9,51
Masters of the Universe 19
men battle men 12
Mera Bharat Mahan 39
Mexico 17,46
Minister for Defence 26
missile attacks 19
mobile phone 48
mobile republic 30
Morocco 46
mosques 48
MTV 25
Nagaland 34
Narmada 46
national consensus 50
'National Identity' 39
National Movement 41
National Pride Parade 29

nationalism tests 26
Nepal 17
newspaper editorials 25
New York 23
non-vedic 45
North America 47
North Korea 17
Norway 17
Nostradamus' predictions 28
Not Knowing What to Believe 18
nuclear bomb 16,26,28,30,50,53
nuclear bondage 32
nuclear button 52
nuclear irradiation 17
nuclear missiles 44
nuclear non-proliferation treaty 30
nuclear plants 13
nuclear posturing 15
nuclear technology 18
nuclear tests 32,44
nuclear test ban treaty 30
nuclear war 11,12,13,17,20,29
nuclear weapons 10,14,19
opinion polls 52
Pakistan 9,11,17,20,26,32,33,34
paper napkin speech 24
Partition 41
Pepsi 44
Peru 46
Petty trouble-maker 19
Pokhran 9,17
Potatoes 46
powdered milk 13
prasad 17
President, US 33,37
Private arsenel 18
Punjab 34
purveyors of madness 19
Radio active fallout 13,34,50
radio active sand 17
Rajasthan 34
Rahim 40

Rashtrapati Bhavan 48
rats 13
Real Indian 49
'Road to Resurgence' 26
rumour-monger 19
Russian roulette 18
Sardar Sarovar 46
Saudi Arabia 17
Second world war 15
Shiv Sena 26
Singapore 17
slavery 34
South Korea 17
Sri Lanka 17
suicide bomber-psyche 16
Super power 35,36
Sweden 17
tea 46, 47
temples 48
Thackeray, Mr 26
the fear of annihilation 15
The God of Small Things 21, 30
The Indian Express 27,28

Theory of Deterrence 15,17
The Pioneer 13
The Times of India 28
thermal blasts 50
Third World War 15
time capsule 50
tobacco 47
tomatoes 46
tribal people 46
Tripura 34
TV chat shows 25
UNDP 36
United States of
    America 12,19,48
Uttarakhand 34
Uzbekistan 17
Vedas 45
VHP 17
Viagra 26
Vietnam 17
Western Culture 44,45
Western Hypocrisy 32,34
White sugar 46